Ampermanager

Amper Soft & DOS Manager

by *Rick Sutcliffe*

Produced by:
Brian Wiser & Bill Martens

 Apple PugetSound Program Library Exchange

Ampermanager: Amper Soft & DOS Manager

www.callapple.org

ISBN: 978-1-71672-307-0

ACKNOWLEDGEMENTS

Ampermanager was programmed by Rick Sutcliffe in 1983, originally published by A.P.P.L.E. in 1983, and is copyright Arjay Enterprises.

This new manual is part of the A.P.P.L.E.-provided portion of the *Ampermanager* package and as such is copyright by A.P.P.L.E.. No claim to copyright over the *Ampermanager* software is created outside of those portions created by A.P.P.L.E..

The Cover and Book were designed by Brian Wiser.

PRODUCTION

Brian Wiser   →   Cover, Design, Layout, Editing
Bill Martens   →   Scanning, Editing, Disk Updates

DISCLAIMER

About Rick Sutcliffe

Rick Sutcliffe, (a.k.a. The Northern Spy) is professor of Computing Science and Mathematics at Canada's Trinity Western University. He has been involved as a member or consultant with the boards of several communities and organizations, and participated in developing industry standards at the national and international level.

Rick has been a mainstay in the Modula-2 and A.P.P.L.E. worlds for more than 35 years. He is a co-author of the Modula-2 programming language R10 dialect. Additionally, he is a long time technology author and has written two textbooks and nine alternate history science fiction novels, one named best ePublished science fiction novel for 2003.

His columns have appeared in numerous magazines and newspapers (paper and online), and he's a regular speaker at churches, schools, academic meetings, and conferences. His "Northern Spy" column has made regular appearances in *Call-A.P.P.L.E.* magazine.

He and his wife Joyce have lived in the Aldergrove/Bradner area of British Columbia, Canada since 1972.

About the Producers

Brian Wiser

Brian Wiser is a long-time consultant, enthusiast and historian of Apple, the Apple II and Macintosh. Steve Wozniak and Steve Jobs, as well as *Creative Computing, Nibble, InCider,* and *A+* magazines were early influences.

Brian designed, edited, and co-produced many books including: *Nibble Viewpoints: Business Insights From The Computing Revolution, Cyber Jack: The Adventures of Robert Clardy and Synergistic Software, Synergistic Software: The Early Games, The Colossal Computer Cartoon Book: Enhanced Edition, What's Where in the Apple: Enhanced Edition, Graphically Speaking: Enhanced Edition,* and *The WOZPAK: Special Edition* – an important Apple II historical book with Steve Wozniak's restored original, technical handwritten notes.

He passionately preserves and archives all facets of Apple's history, and noteworthy related companies such as Beagle Bros and Applied Engineering, featured on AppleArchives.com. His writing, interviews and books are featured on the technology news site CallApple.org and in *Call-A.P.P.L.E.* magazine that he co-produces. Brian also co-produced the retro iOS game *Structris*.

In 2005, Brian was cast as an extra in Joss Whedon's movie *Serenity*, leading him to being a producer and director for the documentary film *Done The Impossible: The Fans' Tale of Firefly & Serenity*. He brought some of the *Firefly* cast aboard his Browncoat Cruise and recruited several of the *Firefly* cast to appear in a film for charity. Brian speaks about his adventures to large audiences at conventions around the country.

Bill Martens

Bill Martens is a systems engineer specializing in office infrastructures and has been programming since 1976. The DEC PDP 11/40 with ASR-33 Teletypes and CRT's were his first computing platforms with his first forays in the Apple world coming with the Apple II computer.

Influences in Bill's computing life came from *Byte* magazine, *Creative Computing* magazine, and *Call-A.P.P.L.E.* magazine as well as his mentors Samuel Perkins, Don Williams, Joff Morgan, and Mike Christensen.

Bill is a co-producer of many books including *What's Where in the Apple: Enhanced Edition, The WOZPAK: Special Edition, Nibble Viewpoints: Business Insights From The Computing Revolution,* and co-programmer for the iOS version of the retro game *Structris*. He has written many articles which have appeared in user group newsletters and magazines such as *Call-A.P.P.L.E.*.

Bill worked for Apple Pugetsound Program Library Exchange (A.P.P.L.E.) under Val Golding and Dick Hubert as a data manager and programmer in the 1980s, and is the current president of the A.P.P.L.E. user group established in 1978. He reorganized A.P.P.L.E. and restarted *Call-A.P.P.L.E.* magazine in 2002. He is the production editor for the A.P.P.L.E. website CallApple.org, writes science fiction novels in his spare time, and is a retired semi-pro football player.

CONTENTS

6. ASDM Applesoft Utilities 17

11. Memory Utilities

12. Management Facilities

```
THE AMPER (SOFT&DOS) MANAGER
      BY  R. SUTCLIFFE
  PRODOS  VERSION  2.1GS
  COPYRIGHT 1983,84,87


                           PTL
```

GETTING STARTED

ASDM (Amper Soft & DOS Manager) requires an Apple II, Apple II Plus, or Apple IIe with at least 48K of RAM. As ASDM is an Applesoft utility, it will not work unless you have Applesoft either in ROM or on a RAM card.

None of the current versions of ASDM will work with DOS on the Language Card.

If you boot the *Ampermanager* 2.1 disk, you will arrive at the Applesoft prompt. This disk is a programmer's disk which allows you to start using Ampersoft commands right away.

If you boot the ASDM disk, either 1.5 or 2.0, the greeting program will automatically initialize the machine language program *Ampermanager*. See the first chapter for a description of your choices at this point.

On the other hand, if you have DOS up and running first SAVE your Applesoft program, then type:

BRUN AMPERMANAGER

If you BRUN Ampermanager, a page of copyright information will appear on your screen.

If you initialize *Ampermanager* from an Applesoft program, the copyright message will be suppressed.

When the program is installed you will be able to use any of the commands in this manual in addition to all normal DOS and Applesoft commands.

Ampermanager will be removed by the commands FP and INT. BRUNning any program affecting low memory ($803- $2150) will overwrite *Ampermanager* and it will have to be reloaded.

Furthermore, they leave the reset vector pointed to the middle of *Ampermanager* and this will soon cause big problems. The correct way to "unhook" the package is to type &NOT&. This gives back all the page three vectors to DOS and does a cold start of DOS, turning off any peripherals such as 80-column cards. Be certain your program is SAVEd first.

The pointers for Applesoft programs are above AMPERMANAGER so that BASIC programs will run as normal.

PLE and *PGE* run at high memory and are not affected by *Ampermanager*.

In the ProDOS versions of *Ampermanager*, the FMTDSK command is disabled due to the fact that FMTDSK is designed for DOS 3.3 5.25" floppy disks and not for larger volume drives.

There are many other commands which are also not available in versions 2.0 and 2.1 because the focus of the commands is DOS-oriented.

See Appendix 1 for alternate initialization schemes.

THE ASDM
APPLESOFT PROGRAMS

Three Applesoft programs included on the *Ampermanager* disk that are included for two purposes: to be used as utility programs, and to serve as demonstrations of the power of *Ampermanager*. The disk image is available from: www.callapple.org.

If you have booted the ASDM disk or run the Greeting program (The Receptionist), you will have a choice of exiting to DOS with *Ampermanager* up and active, or entering one of three Applesoft driver programs.

Each of these three may be RUN independently of *The Receptionist*. If this is done, BRUN AMPERMANAGER first. Even if you forget, each of the three driver programs can load another version of *Ampermanager* at high memory and carry on. See Appendix 1.

```
RECEPTIONIST 2.0          COPYRIGHT 1984
            BY R. SUTCLIFFE

                    MENU

DO YOU WANT TO...

        1) USE THE DOS 3.3 VERSION
        2) LIST SOME INSTRUCTIONS
        3) RUN THE.EXECUTIVE
        4) CATALOG THE DISK
        5) TOGGLE 40/80 COLUMN DISPLAY
        6) EXIT TO PRODOS AND BASIC

....ANSWER HERE===>
```

2.1. The Executive

```
                    THE  EXECUTIVE
COPYRIGHT 1982              BY R.SUTCLIFFE
       1983, 1984

                    MENU

     1) READ FILE FROM DISK
     2) WRITE FILE TO DISK
     3) ADD TO EXISTING FILE
     4) SWAP STATEMENTS IN FILE
     5) LIST FILE
     6) DELETE FROM FILE
     7) START NEW FILE
     8) CATALOG
     9) EXIT TO MAIN MENU
    10) EXIT TO DOS

PICK ONE 1- 10 ?※
```

The purpose of this program is to help you write EXEC files of moderate length (like MAKE TEXT on the DOS 3.3 System Master disk).

You enter the commands you wish to be part of the EXEC file one at a time, and the program creates the file on the diskette when you're done. During the process you can swap lines around, add new ones anywhere in the sequence, or delete lines. If you are writing very large EXEC files, a word processor is better than this simple text organizer.

2.2. The Disk Director

The Disk Director operates many of the *Ampermanager* commands from within a BASIC environment using menus and prompts for user friendliness. You may find the programming examples and techniques used in this program extremely valuable in your use of *Ampermanager*.

In this program, most of the action is centered on the Directory track (17 or $11), for the two main sections are those which allow you to sort the CATALOG into any order you wish, and to write titles into that CATALOG to provide copyright information and "pretty

4

things up" a little. By the way, you can switch freely back and forth between these two sections via the program menu without losing any information – as long as you don't respond "Y" when asked if you want to start a new CATALOG at any time. You can even write the modified CATALOG back to the disk, work on it some more, and write it again.

```
         THE DISK DIRECTOR
           BY R. SUTCLIFFE

              MENU

  1) INIT DISK        10) UNLOCK
  2) FREE DOS TRKS    11) DELETE
  3) TRIM CATALOG     12) RELETE
  4) READ SECTOR      13) TITLE THE CATALOG
  5) ZAP BUFFER       14) VOL/SPACE INFO
  6) WRITE SECTOR     15) RESET SLOT/DRIVE
  7) CATALOG          16) EXIT TO MAIN MENU
  8) SORT CATALOG     17) EXIT TO DOS
  9) LOCK

 PLEASE CHOOSE BY NUMBER ===>※
```

Some of the features built into these two routines are:

- Sorting can be alphabetical or by file type.

- You can set "sorting limits" so that only a portion of the CATALOG is sorted.

- You can exempt the greeting program from the sort so that it appears first.

- Titles can be sorted to the top if you wish.

- Titles can be entered in inverse, flashing, or normal.

- They can be centered or left justified (no file header shows), or they can be lined up with the other CATALOG entries (in which case the header *T 000 will show).

- You can place a border around a section of titles, and you have a choice of what character you wish to use as a border.

5

- You can place the unformatted titles into a "Stock Set" and save this to a disk (NOT the disk you are currently working on, but another one), then retrieve any of these title sets for instant use at any time.

- The titles created can be FIDed to another disk, but if you do this, each will get its own track/sector list sector rather than all using the same one. By the way, the sector actually used is obtained by checking the CATALOG to see if it already has titles, and if so uses their sector. If not, it opens a temporary, dummy file to get one. This file will not be in the final version of the CATALOG but the sector so obtained will be locked out of the VTOC and all the titles will use it.

WARNINGS

Do not save any file, including a stock set of titles to the working disk between the time you start changing its CATALOG around and the time you write it back. Such a file would not appear in the final version of the directory, because it was missing from the one kept in RAM for sorting and titling.

Use a backup copy of your disk for these routines. You take a tremendous risk if you plan to alter the directory on the original disk.

There are INIT (diskette initialization) options that provide for:

- Initializing a disk with DOS and a directory (normal INIT).

- Initializing a disk with just a directory (a diskette with no DOS provides more room for files.

- Initializing a disk with no DOS and no directory.

In addition, simple disk functions such as LOCK, UNLOCK, DELETE, and RELETE (undelete) are provided. Please observe the cautions provided with the latter if you need this option. Note that unlike some other undeleting programs, *Ampermanager* will automatically fix up the VTOC if you have not saved a program over the deleted one.

The Disk Director will also drive *Ampermanager's* various DOS

CATALOGS without interfering with the one stored in RAM and still another option will provide you with volume and space information.

2.3. **The DOS Operator**

Many of the options offered here are the same as in the previous program. For those that do appear to be the same on the menu, the only differences are that no RAM CATALOG is maintained, and the disk formatting routines format the tracks first, then add DOS and/ or CATALOG. The initialization routines are capable of initializing a range of tracks, or even a single track (all using *Ampermanager* commands).

The main difference between the DOS Operator and the Disk Director is the operation of the *Ampermanager* SCAN commands to find bad sectors on your disk, and its ability to change DOS commands, error messages, and the heading 'DISK VOLUME' to suit your own purposes.

Other options in the DOS Operator include a lower case patch for DOS and boot programs which will BRUN or EXEC a file. The option to put DOS on a disk allows you to change the greeting program name or type on any disk. THIS OPTION DOES NOT INITIALIZE THE DISK; it just writes DOS on the first three tracks.

2.4. **Notes (for all three programs)**

The Applesoft extensions described in the rest of this manual are freely used in these programs. Feel free to browse for examples of PRINT USR and other unique features available to you in Ampermanager.

The printer initialization line is 15660. It is currently set up for a Centronics printer, but can be easily configured for your printer.

When RUN from The Receptionist, all three programs offer an exit option of transferring back to Receptionist level. This choice is not offered if the program has been RUN from DOS unless you do a POKE 256,1 first.

You will notice that the copyright information is suppressed when location 256 contains a 1.

Since the menus and instructions are written with a 40-column screen in mind, 80-column screens are explicitly turned off in line 5. This line is the correct way to turn off the Apple IIe 80-column display.

3

AMPERMANAGER INTRODUCTION

The purpose of the remaining portion of this manual is to describe the commands that control *Ampermanager*. Here's how it works:

The Applesoft language contains a command which is just an ampersand (&). This command causes the computer to execute a jump to the memory location $3F5.

A normal boot stores 4C 58 FF in the locations $3F5 to $3F7. This is simply a jump to $FF58 at which address is stored $60 causing the machine language equivalent of the Applesoft command RETURN. The net effect: nothing happens at all!

If we change $3F5 to jump elsewhere, we can write a machine language program which can be entered with an & command.

Such programs are now quite commonplace. Indeed, this has become the most popular way to "hook in" a machine language routine to Applesoft. Without some additional effort, only one program at a time could be entered this way, and since a typical user might want several available at a time, the command CALL was needed to use them.

Ampermanager changes that in two ways:

  – It contains a variety of typical programs which the user might want to access from BASIC, all of which can be called by & <command>.

- It can manage up to 12 other programs in addition to those supplied, allowing the user to enter any of them with simple keyboard commands. This is the management function of the program.

In the following pages, you will find the major management and command features of *Ampermanager*.

CAUTION: Some of the DOS related commands are capable of changing (and destroying) individual tracks and sectors on the disk. Use them on a backup copy, rather than an original diskette.

4

SHORTHAND
APPLESOFT COMMANDS

4.1. Screen Utilities

The following screen utilities are designed for 40-columns. They won't necessarily work if an 80-column text card is active.

```
&I   =   INVERSE
&F   =   FLASH
&N   =   NORMAL
```

These are identical to their long (BASIC) forms, but are easier to type. They do however occupy 2 bytes of memory each rather than 1.

```
&T   =   TRACE
&TX  =   NO TRACE
```

These two are also the same as in BASIC.

&S   =   Show control characters in inverse.

&SX =   Do not show control characters.

The Show command is useful for finding control characters in catalogs and in program listings. Users should be aware that DOS commands may not behave correctly with TRACE or Show in effect.

&WN =   Set narrow window (same as POKE 33 ,33)

&W   =   Initialize wide open text window and text mode.

This last command can be used to return from graphics or to reverse the effect of changing the text windows to a smaller than usual pattern. The only difference between typing & W, and TEXT is that if you happen to be using text Page 2, you will not be returned to text Page 1.

4.2. **The Lower Case Utility**

This utility can only be fully utilized if you have already installed a lower case chip in place of the character generator supplied with your Apple II.

Since this utility uses the input "hooks," it may be incompatible with certain I/O devices such as 80-column cards, as these devices use the same hooks.

&LC initializes this mode.

You can tell that you are in lower case mode by the fact that the cursor no longer flashes. A large cursor indicates upper case and a small one lower case. Since the Apple II does not really "read" the shift key (under normal circumstances), the ESCape key has been used to toggle case.

If you press the ESC key twice, you will be placed in upper case, or shift lock mode. To exit shift lock mode, press the ESC key once.

If you want to capitalize the first letter of a word, then resume input in lower case, simply depress the ESC key once (from shift unlock mode).

If your machine has been modified to recognize the shift key (see Appendix 2), it will work much like the shift key on a normal typewriter when this mode is enabled. In such a case, upper case lock is achieved either as described above, or by pressing <ESC> and the shift key at the same time.

While in this mode, the <ESC> key cannot be used for the normal screen editing, so for these purposes it is replaced by <Ctrl-A>. Simply type <Ctrl-A> in the same way as you would normally use the <ESC> key and follow it by any <ESC> code key that is normally valid on your machine. (For example, <Ctrl-A> followed by B will backspace the cursor.)

Owners of machines with a proper shift key, such as the Apple IIe, Basis 108, and Franklin should note that this utility is compatible with your machine, but the *Ampermanager* lower case mode itself should not be used, as it is less convenient than your keyboard. The utilities described in Appendix 2 which are available in this mode all work, however.

In order to ensure that the <ESC> and game I/O methods of shifting are not enabled on such machines, the ROM is tested for the "signature" bytes. If the proper bytes for an Apple IIe or a Franklin are found, the <ESC> and game I/O shift method is automatically disabled in favor of the true upper/lower case capability.

If you wish to override this process, type this to force the <ESC> or game I/O lower case mode:

```
& LC+
```

If you want to utilize the enhanced input features, but have no lower case capability, you may type:

```
& LC-
```

This command does not enable lower case, but it does enable all the enhanced input commands described in Appendix 2.

To return to normal keyboard mode (all capital letters), type:

```
<Ctrl-N>
```

See Appendix 2 for additional commands you can type while in this mode.

4.3. Miscellaneous Utilities

&M = Go to the Monitor (same as a CALL -151).

&* = Go to the "pseudo-Monitor"

You will receive the prompt "&" and you may now execute one monitor command line, after which you will be returned immediately to BASIC. This even works on the Basis 108 in 80-column mode, but caution should be exercised, as the monitor commands are not all the same.

From either of these, <Ctrl-C> will return to BASIC immediately, and <Ctrl-Y> will return to a running program. If you type <Ctrl-Y> when no program is running, a SYNTAX ERROR will result.

&VR Gives the version number of *Ampermanager*. Pointers for the start and end of programs are not affected by this command.

Definitions
of Conventions

For the following command discussions, we will use the conventions described below to indicate different types of data.

decbyte: a decimal number between 0 and 255

decword: a decimal number between 0 and 65535

hexbyte: a one byte hexadecimal number between $0 and $FF

hexnum: a two byte hexadecimal number between $0 and $FFFF

adrsexp: a hexnum, hexstring or decword (example of hexstring: A$="$C000")

stringexp: a legitimate string expression such as MID$, LEFT$, RIGHT$, etc. For example MID$(A$,5,3).

Any item on a command line enclosed in the symbols < > is optional, and has a special meaning if included. For example: & PEEK (hexnum)<#> means that you need not include the "#", but if you do, it will have special significance. Examples of the two forms of the command are:

```
& PEEK ( $300 )
& PEEK ( $300 )#
```

6

ASDM
Applesoft Utilities

6.1. & WAIT decbyte

This command pauses for decbyte tenths of a second, or until a key is pressed. If premature termination of the WAIT occurs due to a keypress, the number of tenths of a second left in the original specification is placed in memory location 253 ($FD), and the ASCII value of the key that was pressed is placed in location 254 ($FE). For example, if the command:

```
& WAIT 100
```

were issued, and the user pressed the <ESC> key after 1.5 seconds, the value 85 would be placed in location 253, and the value 155 would be placed in location 254.

The ASCII value is stored with the high bit set, so the actual value of the character is obtained by subtracting 128 from the contents of location 254.

6.2. & BEEP decbyte, decword

This beeps the speaker and cassette outputs at a pitch of decbyte for a duration of decword.

6.3. & $hexnum

This command outputs hexnum in decimal. The one Applesoft token that may be formed by the hexadecimal number is ignored, and interpreted properly. For example, the hex number $DEF1 would appear in a program as $ DEF 1, as DEF is an Applesoft word.

6.4. & %decword expression

This outputs decword expression in hexadecimal.

6.5. & FIX

This is Apple's *Redbook* routine for making repairs to the stack. Do this as part of an ONERR routine.

6.6. & SWAP var 1, var 2

This trades the values of two variables. This alleviates garbage collection problems in such procedures as sorting.

6.7. & MOVE stringexp, adrsexp

This copies the string expression at the specified address. The new address should not overlap the original string. For example, to move a string to the text page, type:

```
& MOVE "ABCD1234",1024.
```

6.8. & REV stringexp

This reverses the string expression character by character. For example, this prints "ACBD":

```
10  A$ = "ABCD"
20  & REV MID$(A$,2,2)
30  PRINT A$
```

6.9. & LET stringexp 1=stringexp 2

This substitutes as much of the second string expression as possible into the first, maintaining the length of the first string, which of course must already exist. For example:

```
A$="THIS IS A STRING"

B$="ONGE"

&LET MID$(A$,14,3) = MID$(B$,1,3)
```

A$ now contains the string "THIS IS A STRONG"

The length of the second string or string expression must not exceed the total length of the first string expression.

An illegal use of &LET would be (assuming the same A$ and B$ as above):
```
&LET MID$(A$,14,3)=MID$(B$,1,4)
```

because you are trying to force 4 characters into the space of three. If the space provided is larger than needed, the substitution begins from the leftmost character.

The alternate form for & LET is simply &. For example:

```
& A$ = C$ is equivalent to & LET A$ = C$
```

6.10. & LET stringexp=adrsexp, <hexbyte or decbyte>

This creates a new string descriptor pointing to adrsexp with the length specified by hexbyte or decbyte. If the length is omitted, *Ampermanager* will attempt to compute one by ending the string with the first character after the address which has the high bit set. This is useful for changing DOS or other command tables. For example:

```
&LET A$ $A884,4
```

6.11. & LET variable = adrsexp

This sets the variable to the specified 2 byte integer. For example, this assigns the variable A the value 41395:

```
&LET A=$A1B3
```

6.12. & LET variable= PEEK (adrsexp) <#>

This form of & LET sets the variable to the value at the specified address. If the optional marker, "I" is added immediately after the closing parenthesis, a 16-bit (low, high) PEEK is performed. For example:

```
& LET B PEEK ($43E9)
```

sets B to the 8-bit value contained in memory location $43E9.

```
& LET B = PEEK (1002) #
```

is equivalent to the normal Applesoft statement:

```
B = PEEK (1002) + PEEK (1003) * 256
```

6.13. & LET variable = IN#$ (<offset>,source,target)

This form of the & LET command searches the source string for the first occurrence of the target string. Variable is set to the starting position of the target string, if found. If the source string does not contain the target string, the variable is set to zero.

The offset, if specified, determines the point in the source string at which to begin the scan. If the offset is greater than the length of the source string, an error occurs. Examples:

If A$="123123" and B$="23" then

```
IN#$ ( A$, B$ )          returns 2
IN#$ ( 3, A$, B$ )       returns 5
IN#$ ( 7, A$, B$ )       results in ?DATA ERROR
```

6.14. & GOTO linnumexp

6.15. & GOSUB linnumexp

These two routines allow computed GOTO's and GOSUB's as in Integer BASIC. For example, this transfers control to the subroutine at line number 510:

```
A = 50
&GOSUB 10*A+10
```

6.16. & INPUT "optional message string"; strvariable

This works just like the Applesoft INPUT except that the semicolon will suppress the normal question mark whether it is used with the string message or not, and any string (including commas, quotes or whatever) can be input. Obviously multiple input cannot be done.

6.17. & CRT<;> stringexp, decbyte

This converts the actual characters stored in the string to a different format as specified by decbyte. The Apple actually stores strings partly in "flashing" and partly in "inverse" screen characters, regardless of how they may be printed. Decbyte has the following effect: (see the *Apple II Reference Manual,* page 15)

Decbyte	Effect
0	Letters to lower case (hi-above $E0) numbers to normal
1	To Normal
2	To Flash
3	To Inverse
4	Letters to lower case (lo-$60 to $7F) numbers to normal (LC is rather useless if you have no lower case adaptor)

Once characters are entirely in Inverse or Flashing format, you must inform CRT of this if you change them again or they will become control characters (which never convert) or lower case (instead of numbers). So if this is the case, add 128 to decbyte when converting again.

The purpose of the optional semicolon is to distinguish the & CRT command from the & CRTP command in the rare case that the variable begins with a P. The semicolon need never be included otherwise.

To see the effects use the &?* string option. Try the following examples:

```
A$ = "123ABC" : &? * A$ : & CRT A$,1 : &? * A$
& CRT MID$(A$,2,3),3 : &? * A$
```

6.18. **& CRTP** <linenumber range>, [+/-]<offset>

Converts all strings in the specified line number range to upper case (+) or to lower case (-), skipping <offset> number of characters in each string.

Variable names are not converted unless the command is given as & CRTPV. The offset option in the & CRTPV command applies only to strings, not variables, so all letters in variables will be converted to the specified case. This routine is handy for conversion of programs written on the Apple IIe, Franklin, or Basis-108 to normal Applesoft BASIC.

The line number range uses the LIST syntax. It must be followed by a comma. If no range is specified (just the comma) the whole program is converted.

The + or - is necessary or nothing happens.

The offset is optional. If given, it is usually 1. No problems should occur if it is greater than the length of the string being converted. If the offset is 255, all strings will be skipped in their entirety. For example:

```
& CRTP 10-30 ,-1
```

will convert all but the first character of every string in lines 10 through 30 to lower case.

```
& CRTP,+
```

will convert the whole program to upper case.

```
& CRTPV,+255
```

will convert only the variable names to upper case.

6.19. & POKE adrsexp, value

This puts the low byte of value into the memory location adrsexp, and the high byte of value into memory location adrsexp+l (if value is greater than 255).

If A$ = "$300" and B$ = "A0" then this has the same effect:

```
& POKE A$, B$
& POKE $300, $A0
& POKE 768, B$
& POKE $300, 160
& POKE 768, 160
```

You can poke a whole machine language subroutine using additional commas. For example, this stores a JMP $FF69 at $300:

```
& POKE $300, $4C, $69, 255
```

If one of the numbers being poked has 2 bytes, both will be used in the order low byte then high byte. The above example could be done:

```
& POKE $300,$4C,$FF69
```

6.20. & CALL adrsexp

This is the same as the Applesoft CALL but you can use hex numbers or strings for the argument. This command works like the "G" command in the monitor in that it loads the A, X, Y, and P registers from locations $45 through $48 before jumping to the specified address. The new contents of those registers are loaded into locations $45 through $48 before control is returned to the user. These locations may be set up prior to the CALL using the & POKE command, and examined afterwards using the & REG command. For example:

```
& CALL $300
        or
& CALL A$
```

where A$ = "$300" have the same effect as CALL 768.

6.21. & G

This forces Applesoft to do a garbage collection. Used occasionally throughout a program, it prevents the buildup of a lot of garbage strings.

6.22. & LL (long list)

This is an abbreviation for the ordinary Applesoft LIST command.

6.23. & L (condensed list)

This command will list the program or a range of the program without most of the extra blanks which the ordinary LIST produces. This is useful for editing, especially in long lines containing strings.

6.24. & LF (formatted list)

In this version of LIST a formatted listing resembling that of Pascal is produced. This is useful for documenting programs for others and for finding errors.

For the three list commands, use the standard line number range list as you would in a normal Applesoft LIST command. The following are valid:

```
& L 10,100
& LL 50-200
& LF 210
& L 20-
```

The condensed list and the formatted list can be paused with any key or terminated by <Ctrl-C>.

6.25. **& RESTORE** linnum expression

This command will restore the DATA pointer to the first DATA element on or after the specified line number (you may use a constant, a variable, or an expression to specify the line number). A SYNTAX ERROR results if no number is specified.

7

Extended PRINT Statement

This is another Applesoft extension, but it has many options and deserves a section of its own.

The command is invoked by & ? or & PRINT followed by whatever syntax is desired.

In normal Applesoft as well as *Ampermanager,* the reserved word "PRINT" is interchangeable with the question mark(?). When listed, the question mark expands to the word "PRINT". In most of the examples below, we have chosen the question mark notation. Typing in the word "PRINT" will work identically.

All options available in the Applesoft PRINT are still available and work in exactly the same way except for the comma which tabs only in eight space fields instead of normal sixteen provided by Applesoft.

The & PRINT TAB works correctly on the Apple IIe 80-column card, as do comma tabs. They do not work at all in the Applesoft PRINT statement when the 80-column card is active.

In addition, the following key symbols are used to specify various options to & PRINT (pronounced amper-print).

7.1. Literal Printing: &? *

All strings in the PRINT statement from the first asterisk(*) to the end of the line or to a second asterisk will be printed as stored – i.e.

without setting the high bit. For example:

```
A$="ABC123":  &?*A$
```

outputs A$ literally as stored.

```
&?  B$;*A$*;C$
```

outputs B$ and C$ normally and A$ literally.

The semicolons (;) are not always required, but may be necessary to prevent the asterisk (*) from being interpreted as a multiplication operator.

7.2. Repeat Printing: &? (decbyte)

The next string or the material between two delimiters or between a delimiter and the end of the line will be printed (decbyte) times (up to 255). Only the apostrophe may be a delimiter. For example:

```
&?(10)A$
```

outputs A$ ten times.

```
&?(11)'A$,10,
```

outputs A$ and the number ten in appropriate tab fields eleven times. The last comma is to force a tab after the 10.

```
&?(5)*'A$'3
```

outputs A$ literally five times, then the number 3 once.

If a literal (*) marker is inside a repeat field, be sure to turn off the literal with another (*) before the repeat delimiter('). If the literal field is not closed off in this manner, you will get alternately literal and normal printing as each asterisk serves to toggle the literal mode.

7.3. Screen Management:
&? AT(decbyte,decbyte)

Does an ordinary HTAB and VTAB within the PRINT statement for the next output. This command will work on the Apple IIe's 80-column screen even though the normal Applesoft HTAB command will not. For example:

```
&? AT (3,7) A
```

does HTAB 3 and VTAB 7, then outputs the value of A.

7.4. Decimal to Hex Printing: &? %

Outputs a decimal input as a hex number. For example, this results in 0A and a hex representation of the value of B, respectively:

```
&?%10 and &?%B
```


7.5. Printing Contents of Memory:
&? PEEK (adrsexp)<#>

Works just like the one in Applesoft except for the new types of arguments. If the optional "#" marker is included in the & PEEK command, a 16-bit number is retrieved. For example, if location $300 contains $01, and location $301 contains $02:

```
& PEEK ( $300 )     yields 1
& PEEK ( $300 )#    yields 513 (the 16-bit quantity)
```

If you wish to select the ordinary PEEK, you will have to use it as part of a formula such as &?1*PEEK(M) so that it does not appear first.

7.6. Clear Screen Print: &? HOME

Can be placed anywhere in the extended PRINT line. Obviously though it is really only useful right at the beginning, otherwise you would erase some of your printing before being able to read it. For Example:

```
&?HOME"HELLO"
```

7.7. IN#$ (<offset>, source, target)

This command allows you to print the position of a target string in the source string. For more information on the syntax, see the IN#$ section under & LET.

7.8. Print Using (user formatting): &? USR

This is a full featured PRINT USING command. The proper Syntax is:

```
&? USR string exp, list of expressions
&? USR decbyte, list of expressions
```

In the first syntax, the string expression is a format string, either stored in a variable or used as a quoted string.

In the second syntax, the decbyte specifies the width of the field of blanks to use for the output.

In either syntax, the list of expressions is the data to print according to the specified format. Commas separate elements of the list.

Numerical expressions are rounded off to the number of decimal places indicated by zeros or I holders to the right of the decimal and then printed right-justified in the field. For example:

```
&? USR "**0.00", 3.465, 4.2
```

results in:

```
**3.47  **4.20
```

A number of special characters can be used in a string. Their effect is:

1. The rightmost period is the decimal; any to its left are treated as non-substituting literals.

2. -, Are non-substituting literals. The comma is also used to separate the elements in the list. If it is to be used as a tab instead, terminate the USR portion with a semicolon first.

3. $ Will print where placed but is bumped left if necessary.

4. ^ Four up arrows to the right of the decimal will provide space for an exponent starting with the first one. They should therefore be contiguous.

5. # This is an alternate marker for the right justification in cases where a decimal is not wanted. If no # or decimal is encountered in scanning the string, all entries will be right-justified in the mask.

For example, using the character ␢ (ALT+9250 or U+2422) to indicate a blank:

```
& ? USR "␢␢#␢",12,345
```

```
Results in:    12␢345␢
```

For strings which must be formatted, simply include them in the list after the mask. Numerical expressions and strings may be freely intermixed as long as the print mask you have specified is compatible with both. For example:

```
Statement:  &? USR "␢␢␢#␢␢␢" 123, "ABCD"
Result:     123 ABCD␢␢
```

If you desire the string to be left justified follow it with the letter "L". If it is to be centered in the field, use the letter "C", and if it is to be right-justified, use the letter "R". These specifiers override any justification specified in edit masks.

An exclamation point immediately following the number or string causes a line feed and a tab over to the same vertical position at which the last edit string was printed to be issued. This allows a single PRINT USR command to print in columnar form. For example:

```
If A$ = "**$00.00" and B$ = "  #^^^^"
```

Statement:	&? USR A$, 235.689
Result:	*$235.69

Statement:	&? USR B$, -15.9E10
Result:	-16 E+11

Spaces surrounding the ^ signs come out just as entered.

Statement:	&? USR A$,1.5-E
Result:	>>>>>>>> (overflow)

Statement:	&? USR" .00 ^ ^^^" , 11.56E-5
Result:	11.56 E-05^

The ^ sign appears because the exponent starts at the first of the four places reserved.

Statement:	&?USR "000-000-000", 124769115
Result:	124-769-115

Statement:	&? USR " 0.00","ME"L
Result:	ME 0.00

Statement:	&? USR "ƃ ƃ ƃ#ƃ ƃ ƃ",12,"WW"L!,"MR"C, "ART"R!;5
Result:	ƃ ƃ12ƃ ƃ ƃWW ƃ#ƃ ƃ ƃ
	ƃ ƃMR ƃ ƃ ƃ ƃ ƃ#ART
	5

Notice that the # sign is not removed when using the numeric mask for a literal. The 5 is not printed in a mask because it is preceded by the semicolon (;) which terminates the USR portion of the extended print statement.

8

PRINTER UTILITY

Syntax:

```
& P <slot number>,<,printer setup string expression>
```

This utility turns on the output device in the specified slot and sends the specified setup string to it. *Ampermanager* "remembers" the last specified setup string, so if the setup string is omitted, the last one used (if any) is sent.

The default slot number is 1, so if your printer is in Slot 1, & P will turn it on. The last specified slot is "remembered" just as the last setup string, so & P is all that is necessary after the first call.

You can even BSAVE a copy of *Ampermanager* with your default setup string so you never have to type it again.

If there is a control character in your setup string that is not available from the keyboard, simply use the up-arrow (^) key followed by the letter c followed by the letter. For example, to enter a Ctrl-C, simply type: ^CC. To enter an ESC in a sequence, use the code ^E. The up-arrow is a Shift-N on an Apple II, and a Shift-6 on an Apple IIe. For example, assume your printer was in Slot 2, and required the setup string:

```
<RETURN><ESC><Ctrl-T><Ctrl-I>80N
```

You would type:

```
& P 2,"^CM^E<Ctrl-T><Ctrl-I>80N"
```

or:

```
& P 2,"^CM^E^CT^CI80N"
```

In the case of Ctrl-T and Ctrl-I, there is really no harm in typing them from the keyboard, but they will not be visible in your Applesoft programs.

Your finished setup string may not exceed 16 characters. If it does, you will get a ?STRING TOO LONG error.

Other uses for this command are for turning on an 80-column card in Slot 3 (& P 3), or re-booting your system from Slot 6 (& P 6).

DOS Catalogs

9.1. &C – Catalog

&C gives standard CATALOG. The following three can be paused by hitting any key, terminated by <Ctrl-C>.

9.2. &CD – Catalog Deleted Files

&CD catalogs the deleted files only.

9.3. &CC – Continuous Catalog

&CC continuous catalog in a 20 space field with no linefeeds and no pause. If there are no control characters in a catalog two files will fit on a row of the screen or four on an 80-column printer. If control characters mess things up it will be obvious; use &S to print them.

9.4. &CE – Extended Catalog

&CE extended catalog gives standard format including the pause, but adds in Hex the Track then the Sector of the track/sector list and if appropriate, the starting address and length of the file. Unless followed by a suppressing semicolon, all four catalogs fall into the &FRE routine.

9.5. &FRE – Print Free Sectors

&FRE prints the number of free sectors on the disk. (Unlike *FID,* this one works. It should work if used on 40 or 70 track versions as well.)

All five allow D,S,V,A, track/sector options but the last two have no effect.

10

ASDM DOS UTILITIES

WARNING: These utilities are DOS 3.3 compatible. They may not work on patched or relocated versions of DOS, or on DOS 3.2. Use them in these environments at your own risk.

Wherever the words "filename expression" are used in the following discussion, any Applesoft string may be used. Unlike DOS, quotes must surround a name given directly. See the examples.

10.1. **& RELETE** filename expression

Undeletes a file and restores the VTOC (lists as RE LET E in a program).

10.2. **& SWIRD**

Switches the normal DOS DELETE to/from RELETE giving the option of undeleting via a program:

```
& SWIRD:?CHR$(4) "RELETE filename": & SWIRD
```

You would want to use this command for readability (as mentioned above, Applesoft breaks RELETE up into RE LET E), and because DELETE is a normal DOS command and its arguments need not be quoted strings.

10.3. **&DR** – Switch Drives

&DR Switches drives between #1 and #2. If using a controller with more than two drives, use the command &,D<drive#>.

10.4. **&B** – Length and Location of Last BLOAD

&B Tells you where and for what length the last file BLOADed or BRUN was located.

10.5. **& GETB** filename stringexp

Steals a buffer from DOS and opens it under filename. If the user wishes, this buffer can be used, by name, to read or write with the following. See notes 1,4.

10.6. **& READ** optional filename stringexp, tracksector expression

Does GETB or uses the buffer named if a name is provided and reads the specified track and sector into the buffer. See notes 1,2,3,4,5,6.

10.7. **& WRITE** optional filename stringexp, tracksector expression

Likewise, but writes the sector back to the disk. With no parameters, sends back the last sector read. See notes 1,2,3,6.

10.8. **& OPEN** filename stringexp

Finds the specified file on the disk and reads its first sector into a DOS buffer for further examination. See notes 1,4,5.

10.9. & INIT Greeting program string expression<;>

The same as standard INIT but does not save the current Applesoft program under the given name. The result is a normal DOS 3.3 diskette which would boot and try to run the greeting program but would not have it as the Catalog has no files.

This routine continues directly into the & SCAN procedure (documented below), unless followed by the optional semicolon (;)

This is useful if you want to initialize bootable disks with a program but some other program will become the greeting program. See note 1.

10.10. & FMTDSK

Formats the disk without DOS or a directory. This may be useful for some types of data diskettes. See notes 1,8.

10.11. & PUTD Greeting program string expression

Puts DOS onto tracks 0 to 2. This utility assumes that these tracks are available for this purpose. See note 1.

10.12. & PUTV

Creates a new VTOC in Track $11 sector 0, erasing the old one. See note 1.

10.13. & PUTC

Creates a fresh, blank catalog and VTOC in track $11, destroying the original one, and effectively rendering the disk blank.

WARNING: A successful &READ0 to a disk containing a valid VTOC in track $11 sector 0 must precede either of these above two utilities or the new VTOC will not be correct. You may also use one of the catalogs to accomplish this read. See note 1.

10.14. & SCAN

Will scan the entire disk for bad sectors and report their track and sector on the screen.

An S-type file called "BAD SECTORS" will be created in the directory to ensure these are locked out of the track bit map in the VTOC.

This latter action can be suppressed (in order to SCAN a pure text disk) by following the command with a semicolon.

This command can be halted by pressing any key or terminated with <CTRL-C>. If it is halted with a RESET, some patches will remain in DOS and you will have to re-boot.

10.15. & DX

Disconnects DOS. This is equivalent to the DOS commands PR#0:IN#0 when the keyboard and the screen are the I/O devices. If some other I/O device, such as a printer, was being used by DOS, it remains active.

10.16. & D

Reconnects DOS. This is done automatically by all *Ampermanager* routines using DOS or disconnecting it. This includes the &DUMP, &Land &LF commands which turn DOS off to get a faster printout.

10.17. & TYPE filename expression

Will open a text file and print its contents on the screen. This can be quite valuable if you have forgotten what is in a file. See note 1.

NOTES:

1. ,V,D,S are valid with decimal arguments only. (This subroutine can also be accessed from command mode by &, (V,D,S expression.) & ,S5,D2 would change the DOS default drive to Slot 5, Drive 2 for all subsequent *Ampermanager* or DOS commands.

2. , A adrsexp specifies a buffer address instead of the one found by DOS. This option should not be used with filenames as the DOS buffer reserved would not be used. See the warning under note 3.

3. , tracksector expression can be either (,decbyte,decbyte) or (Hexword) (track then sector) or (,hexbyte,hexbyte).

    & READ,17,5 is the same as & READ,1105 or & READ,$11,5

    WARNING: If you use variables for your track and sector expression, they must not start with V,D,S, and especially not with A as the system could hang or read into your program areas.

4. If a buffer is used by name it must be CLOSEd by DOS in the normal way. This is done by typing CLOSE <filename>. If you do not specify a filename, DOS will close all the buffers. If you do not release the buffers in this manner, they will remain active until you run out of buffers and get a DOS error. No disk I/O will take place during this operation because the buffer is merely released in the RAM memory.

5. In direct mode both & READ and & OPEN fall into &DUMP, which is described in the next section. However, this action can be suppressed by following the command with a semicolon. In program mode this action is suppressed unless the command is followed by &.

6. & READ decbyte and & WRITE decbyte are optional modes for these commands.

If decbyte = 0 the VTOC sector is read/written.

If decbyte is between 1 and the maximum sector number (inclusive) then that sector in the directory sequence is read. (eg. 5 reads the fifth catalog sector, etc.)

If decbyte is greater than maximum sector number, then the next sector to the one currently in the catalog buffer is read.

When this is done and the results dumped, the user will notice that a separate buffer is kept by DOS for this purpose. Filenames are therefore not valid in this mode as the buffers in question cannot be reserved.

In addition, since DOS only maintains one buffer for the directory sector, & WRITE followed by a number from 1to127 will write that buffer back to its track and sector.

7. & WRITE either by itself or followed by a number from 128 to 255 will write the last buffer read back to its track and sector, regardless of whether it is the VTOC, directory sector buffer or a data sector.

    If a filename is included with a WRITE (but no other information), then the DATA buffer for that filename is written back to the track and sector from which it came. More than one file can be open and altered before doing this. *Ampermanager* will not lose the track and sector. However, if you have issued a GETB to reserve a buffer, and you WRITE that to the disk by name, it could go anywhere (usually track 0 sector 0) because there is no information stored in memory for that file.

    As a second precaution, please note that the memory locations containing the pointers to the buffer can be changed by other routines, so in most cases it would be a good precaution to note the buffer address when you see the screen dump and use it with the ,A option to ensure the correct memory is written.

8. < ,ON track> <,TO track> are legitimate options and specify the starting and ending track for the formatting. These options are accepted with all the *Ampermanager* DOS commands, but they have no effect on any but the & FMTDSK command

EXAMPLES:

& READ,110F

Will read track $11 sector $0F to a DOS buffer and dump it to the screen.

& READ1;

Is identical to the previous example, but uses a catalog buffer and the dump is suppressed.

& READ1 &

Is identical to the last example but forces the dump, which is not automatic when invoked from an Applesoft program.

& READ,17,15,D1,S5

Is identical to the previous two examples, but specifies a slot and drive.

& INIT "HELLO"

Does a standard INIT but stores no actual program on the diskette.

& FMTDSK, ON4, T09, D1

Formats the fourth through ninth tracks on the disk currently in Drive 1.

& READ "JUNK",D1

Opens a buffer for the file JUNK on the disk in Drive 1, and places the first sector in the file buffer. The contents of this buffer are then dumped to the screen.

MEMORY UTILITIES

11.1. & DUMP adrsexp

Gives a hex dump and interpretation of the 256 bytes starting at the given address.

An 80-column card which uses locations $21 and $24 for the window width and horizontal cursor position (respectively) will give a similar display, but will utilize the entire screen width. The Apple IIe 80-column card, which only utilizes one of the above locations, is also supported.

With no parameters, the last page read by DOS will be dumped. This is fallen into when in direct mode by & READ and & OPEN but has to be involved separately from a program.

Page $C0 cannot be dumped; this is for your protection as you would then be locked out of the computer. Furthermore, if you dump anywhere from page $BF, your dump starts at $BF00.

If the user is in direct mode the starting address of the dump is displayed at the end of the interpretation along with a command line +-Z(OFFSET). At this point, simply type the command you want, followed by <RETURN>.

+   Dumps the next 256 bytes.

-    Dumps the previous 256 bytes.

z   Hexbyte allows you to Zap the buffer beginning with the chosen offset for as many bytes as you want using the Monitor syntax (each byte you type as a replacement must be separated from the last by a space). See the section on the & ZAP command.

For example:

& DUMP $100 followed by Z05 will prompt 0105: and you follow the colon by the new values you want, say 01 05 02 <RET>

When you are done, you will be returned to DUMP to see the results.

A bare carriage return exits DUMP, as does any other key not in the command line.

The following apply only if DUMP has been entered from READ or OPEN.

The hex dump is followed by a four digit number TTSS giving the track and sector of the buffer contents. If from open, a six digit number PPTTSS is used instead, with the first two being the relative sector position in the file (starting at 0).

Two more options are called out on the command line:

< (last sector)
or
> (next sector)

If the ">" or "<" options are called from OPEN, the next or previous relative sector in the file is read and displayed. You cannot read past the beginning or end so if you try the same buffer is dumped again. You are kept informed by PP where you are in the file. If you leave this mode and WRITE this buffer, the correct track and sector for the last sector read will be selected for the write.

If the ">" or "<" options are called from READ , the next or previous sector on the disk is read and displayed. For example, if the current sector is 120F and you issue > the one read and displayed will be 1300.

If the ">" or "<" options are called from READ<digit>, the next or previous sector on the track is read and displayed. Unlike the ordinary READ, this means that if 110E is up a > will give 110D, not

110F ,and the next one after 110F is 1100 (you stay on the directory track).

There are five additional options available which are not called out on the command line. These are:

<Ctrl-T>   Switches the active buffer to that of the track/sector list for this file. The change in the display line at the bottom. The relative sector number is preserved if you OPENed the file, but the track/sector has changed. This would not happen if you had issued a + command to display this information. The difference is that this buffer can now be zapped and THEN WRITTEN BACK TO THE DISK using the ! command below.

<Ctrl-D>   Switches the active buffer back to the data buffer.

!   Writes the active buffer back to its track and sector. This differs from WRITE (without track/sector information) in that WRITE will always select the data buffer if not instructed otherwise. The concept of the active buffer is valid only for this command.

<Ctrl-B>   Clears the buffer being displayed to zeros.

<Ctrl-C>   Exits the DUMP and CLOSEs the buffer. If any other key is pressed, there is also an exit, but the buffer is left reserved under the filename. Eventually, you will run out of buffers if they are not CLOSEd.

11.2. & ZAP optional hexbyte

This command allows you to change the last buffer which was dumped. If that was located at $8600 and you commanded & ZAP20, the program would respond with 8620: and you would then type in the new hex values using the Monitor syntax (one space between each) until done.

When you press a carriage return, the commands are entered and you are sent to DUMP to examine your handiwork. Of course, you can ZAP again from there with Z plus your offset.

While this command is fallen into from DUMP in direct mode, it must be invoked separately from a program. This allows the programmer to write a ZAP with more user prompts and more options.

The default value of this hexbyte argument is zero.

11.3. & REG

This command displays the contents of register memory (locations $45 through $48).

12

Management Facilities

12.1. Automatic

&<   Do old ampersand command

When *Ampermanager* is initialized the existing ampersand vector is stored within it and can be invoked with this command (provided the earlier program has not been overwritten).

For example, if *PGE* were installed before *Ampermanager*, then after initialization, the command &< would operate the Renumber commands.

&>   Do new ampersand command

This works just like &< but is for programs which were BLOADed after *Ampermanager*. For example, if, after setting up *Ampermanager*, you wish to use - the Toolkit APA program, you could type:

```
RUN LOAD APA
NEW
<RESET>
```

and thereafter, access all APA commands with &> (followed by correct syntax)

12.2. Cold-start

To "cold start" *Ampermanager* from Applesoft:

CALL 25 or CALL 2051

From the Monitor:

*803G

or

*19G

If another Ampersand program is BRUN after *Ampermanager* and none of the machine language code has been overwritten, these calls will reinitialize *Ampermanager* intact and will now manage the new program via the &> command (above). However, that a cold-start bombs your Applesoft program and variables.

12.3. Warm-start

Press the <RESET> button. This will re-hook the program without destroying a BASIC program or its variables.

If you decide not to use *Ampermanager* any more, it must be unhooked by the command &NOT& to release the Page 3 vectors back to DOS, perform a cold-start, releasing the I/O hooks at the same time.

12.4. Semi-automatic

There are ten positions within *Ampermanager* where a jump to any part of the Apple memory can be stored at any time by the user.

Setup: These positions are set up by the command & SET digit, address where digit is a number from 0 to 9 and address is a decimal, hexadecimal or hex string. For example:

52

```
& SET 1,768
```

Loads a jump to decimal address 768 into command #1

```
& SET 2,$300
```

Loads the same address into command #2

```
& SET 3,A$
```

Where A$ = "$300" has the same effect

```
& SET10, address
```

Loads the program at address into the command < if that is not
needed for the "old" amper vector.

```
& SET11, address
```

Does likewise for the address normally used for the "new"
ampersand vector (the one invoked by & >).

Use: Once the jump has been SET, it is invoked by the command &
digit, <syntax> where:

- Digit is the same number as in part you SET.
- The comma is necessary.

Any syntax required by the command follows. For example,
if we wrote & SET l,$FF69 then thereafter the command & 1, would
jump to the Monitor.

Defaults:

Ampermanager comes with some built in addresses stored for these digits in case you find them useful.

DIGIT	ADDRESS	PURPOSE
0	$19	Ampermanager re-entry
1	$FF58	just a return, does nothing
2	$208	used to call RBOOT
3	$300	standard Page 3 entry
4	$3D0	DOS warms tart
5	$970C	PLE re-entry
6	$8D00	CRAE/PGE re-entry
7	$9500	Soft Seventy entry
8	$803	Page 8 entry, use on alternate version
9	$8D55	GHR2 initialization

CAUTIONS: Do not use the jump unless you know where it is going – you could end up lost and wandering somewhere in machine language. It is the user's responsibility to protect LOMEM or HIMEM from program or variables for these additional routines.

12.5. Repeat

&& syntax = do last command again

If you are using one of the longer commands repeatedly just type a double ampersand followed by any syntax the command requires. The second & simply acts as a wildcard for the last command name (including the digit, <, and > commands).

13

DEFAULTS

When Applesoft encounters a command which it does not recognize it will assume it is a new line if it starts with a number, and that it is a LET otherwise.

Ampermanager will assume that a number (other than 0-11) following an & is an integer to convert to hex (the % command) and that otherwise the &LET command has been invoked.

Consequently &16 will result in 10 (hex).

&MID$(A$,5,3,) = MID(B$,2,3,)
will substitute 3 characters from the second of B$ to the fifth of A$.

&A = PEEK ($300)
will set A equal to the value at hex address $300, or $300 and $301, if you use the form & PEEK ($300)*.

A limited effort to foolproof this has been made. For example, &CD = $FF works even though CD is a command because the first few places are checked for the = sign, and if one is found, then LET is assumed.

APPENDIX 1

14.1. Alternate Initialization Schemes

When calling in the *Ampermanager* package from a program, you might not wish the program pointers reset. In this case BLOAD the program, then CALL 2062 ($80E). Of course, unless your Applesoft program starts at $2150 or higher, you will bomb your program.

One way around this is to have a version of *Ampermanager* residing just above HIMEM; this is provided on the program disk as AMPERMANAGER.HI. This program BLOADs and operates at $7CB0 and resets HIMEM.

Since HIMEM is redefined by AMPERMANAGER.HI, string array space is destroyed. Do not BRUN this program from any place but the beginning of an Applesoft program.

In order to prevent the program pointers from being reset, CALL 31931.

For those familiar with R type files, a re-locatable version is also provided as AMPERMANAGER.REL and its loader can be entered into an Applesoft program in the usual way. (Strings are destroyed and HIMEM moved down just enough from DOS or any other user to accommodate *Ampermanager*.)

The user must, in this case, supply RLOAD and RBOOT from their own copy of the Toolkit and write a loader to bring these into memory and execute them.

14.2. Summary of Starting Options

Cold start: Resets program pointers and HIMEM, bombs variables, and issues a copyright notice. Low memory version bombs program as well by doing a NEW. Execute this start by BRUNing *Ampermanager* from direct mode or the monitor, or by CALLing the starting address or issuing a CALL 25

Lukewarm start: Same as above, but does not issue the copyright notice. This is done automatically if the program is BRUN from an Applesoft program. It can also be achieved by a CALL to (starting address + 9), or 2060 for the low memory version.

Warm start: As discussed above, no memory resets or copyright, and you CALL (starting address +11) or hit the RESET button. Remember to give the reset back to DOS by issuing an &NOT& before reusing *Ampermanager's* memory space with a program like *FID* or *COPYA*.

None of the current versions of *Ampermanager* will operate on the Language Card or with DOS on the card. This option may be included in a later version along with &SORT array and perhaps some new Utilities – but don't hold your breath, its already been a lot of work. They will work with the imitation 'Apples' on the market, but may not with a patched DOS, especially if the INIT has been removed, or the text file handlers changed.

Ampermanager is fully compatible with the Apple IIe, and will often work with "imitation Apples." As noted previously, if you patch or relocate DOS (especially if you need to remove the INIT command or rearrange the text file handlers), *Ampermanager* will probably not work.

If you have an 80-column card active, you should avoid use of the *Ampermanager* commands:

        & LC
        & S
        & T

Some care has been taken to ensure compatibility with the slightly different Monitor in the Apple IIe, and with the very different one on the Basis-108. *Ampermanager* should function correctly on those machines in 40 and 80-column modes. This may not be true of an 80-column card on the Apple II Plus, as there is no standard protocol for those cards.

APPENDIX 2

15.1. Lower Case Mode Commands

&LC

Enter Mode. As discussed earlier, the enhancements discussed below are available in both the &LC+ and &LC- modes. On the Basis-108, if you are in full Apple emulation mode, you can use the lower case if you select character set 4 by typing: POKE 49159,0

& LC would then disable the Basis shift key, and enables the <ESC> key case toggle described earlier.

<Ctrl-N>

Leave Mode and warm-start DOS

<Shift-Ctrl-M>

Enter the Monitor

<Ctrl-A>

Replaces <ESC> for screen editing. No functions are added. You have whatever came with your computer and nothing more.

<Ctrl-E>

Prints an <ESC> followed by whatever character you type next. This is useful for sending <ESC> codes to printers. The cursor will vanish while the machine waits for the character you wish to have follow the <ESC>.

<Ctrl-R>

Displays the contents of memory locations $45 through $48 (memory register locations).

Some codes on some printers (especially Centronics machines) must be preceded by a <RET>. Since you already have at least a prompt character on the screen line, this will not work unless the <RET> is also sent at the beginning of the <ESC> code sequence. To accomplish this, type a + sign after <Ctrl-E> and before the character you wish to send.

This command may also be used when you are not in Lease mode by typing &<Ctrl-E><RET>. As in the above mode, the cursor vanishes and you may type your <ESC> code. In this case, a <RET> has just been sent and you will not need another one.

15.2. *Additional Arrow Functions*

`<Ctrl-W>`   Does sixteen right arrows for fast copying of program lines.

`<Ctrl-Q>`   Does eight left arrows for fast backspace deleting in a line. You cannot backspace past the start of the line. As in BASIC, these are screen functions and ignore control characters. If you prefer to 'arrow' faster or slower than eight and sixteen, then use POKE30,N where N is the number of left arrows you want from a <Ctrl-Q>. The number of right arrows is always twice this number N. Location 30 is reset to 8 (the default value) whenever LC mode is entered. The number N should be kept reasonably small and works best as a power of two.

15.3. Special Characters

To obtain one of the special characters, first type <Ctrl-K>, then type K,L,M,N, or O. The character you get depends on whether you are in upper or lower case. It will also vary according to the actual chip you have installed. The following are more or less standard:

```
Key   Upper Case          Lower Case
---   ---------------      -----------------
K     [ left bracket      { left brace
L     \ backslash         | vertical bar
M     ] right bracket     } right brace
N     ↑ up arrow          ~ tilde
O     _ underline         small box or  apple
```

Some of these are not new of course, but if the shift key is being used as such then of course there has to be a way of obtaining the characters that normally are found there – for instance on <SHIFT N>.

The shift key modification referred to involves connecting the non-grounded side of the shift key to the fourth hole in the right side of the game paddle connector-looking from the front. (just press it in, do not solder at this end.) In newer machines, a Radio Shack Micro Test Clip 270-370 attached to the second pin from the right of the keyboard encoder multi pin connector (approximately under the * key) and wired to the game paddle with #22 wire will do the trick. On older machines it is necessary to solder the wire to the bottom of the keyboard itself, a process which requires the computer to be dismantled and which also voids the warranty.

You may modify your Apple IIe to generate the game I/O shift signal in the following manner: either join solder pad S5, or attach one end of a wire to the game paddle connector (as above), and the other end (strip about 2 cm.) to the pin 27 hole of the keyboard connector plug. Bend the keyboard end of the wire around the side of the connector, then plug the keyboard back in.

The advantage of such an arrangement on an Apple IIe is that some of the Apple II Plus word processors absolutely require a "one-wire shift mod." **WARNING:** Soldering or re-wiring your computer is dangerous, so unless you are fairly confident with this procedure, let a trained service person do it.

15.4. Amper Soft Commands

<	; < TO OLDV	SWAP	
>	; > TO NEWV	REV	
F&	; F&	CRT	
NOT&	; not&	MOVE	
WAIT		LET	
BEEP		CALL	
SET	; TO ATTACH PROGRAMS	POKE	
$	; $ FOR HEX ==>DEC	P	; P FOR PRINTER
%	; % FOR DEC ==>HEX	RESTORE	
L	; L FOR LIST	GOTO	
LIST		GOSUB	
LF	; FORMATTED LIST	PRINT	; FOR LCASE
LL	; LONG LIST	INPUT	
M	; M FOR MONITOR	D	; D FOR DOS RECONNECT
REG	; FOR REGS	DX	; FOR DOS OFF
I	; I FOR INVERSE	C	; C FOR CAT
F	; F FOR FLASH	CE	; CE FOR CATALOG
N	; N FOR NORMAL	WRITE	
T	; T FOR TRACE	OPEN	
TX	; TX FOR TRACE OFF	READ	; CATCH LOWER CASE TOO TYPE
W	; W FOR NORMAL WINDOW	,	; COMMA FOR DRIVE,SLOT,ETC
WN	; WN FOR NARROW WINDOW	/	; / FOR PATHNAME
S	; S FOR SHOW SWITCH	DUMP	
SX	; SX FOR NOSHOW	ZAP	; ZAP
V		J	; * FOR PSEUDOMON
LC	; FOR LOWER CASE	VR	; FOR VERSION
85	; CTRL-E FOR ESC SEND		
FIX		* FMTDSK IS DE-ACTIVATED	

15.5. DOS-only Amper Soft Commands

PEEK	; Get Peek of Hex Location
G	; Forces Applesoft to do a Garbage Collection
*	; Now J as of Version 2.1
IN#$	; Print Position of Target String in Source String
URR	; User Formatting
CD	; Catalog Deleted Files
CC	; Continuous Catalog
FRE	; Print Free Sectors (&V in PRODOS)
RELETE	; Undeletes a File
SWIRD	; Switches normal DOS Delete to/from RELETE
DR	; Switch Drives
B	; Length and Location of Last BLOAD
GETB	; Steals a buffer from DOS for File
INIT	; INIT Greeting Program
FMTDSK	; Format disk without DOS or Directory
PUTD	; Put DOS on Tracks 0 to 2
PUTV	; Put VTOC in Track 11 Sector 0
PUTC	; Create a fresh blank catalog
SCAN	; Scan entire disk for Bad Sectors

16

MEMORY USAGE

Users who write their own machine language routines should be aware of what memory locations are utilized by *Ampermanager*. Here is a summary:

Page 0: 6 - 9 and 25 - 27, 30, 31 (from $19) are reserved locations and contain various flags used by the program. They should not be tampered with. In addition, most of the available locations from 224-255 are used for scratch. Graphics commands use some of these, so you could lose some information for those routines when you issue an *Ampermanager* command. The I/O hooks are stolen only when the Lower Case input is on.

Page 1: 256 is used to store a flag when invoking the Applesoft programs in the package. This suppresses copyright information in those programs. This page also contains the stack, which must be manipulated by the Lower Case input routines.

Page 3: The Reset, Ampersand, and Monitor (Ctrl-Y) vectors are all used. The &NOT& command restores them to DOS.

Ampermanager: The program stores one flag internally. This tells it if LC mode should be entered on the RESET cycle (including whether it is in LC- mode). If you RESET in this mode, you stay in it. The default cycle does not enter LC mode, say on BRUNning the program, but this can be changed. Just BSAVE a copy of the program when LC mode is on, and when that copy is BRUN it will come up in LC mode. The printer setup string is stored internally to *Ampermanager* so it can be BSAVEd with a copy of *Ampermanager*.

Ampermanager   Uses $803 to $2150

Ampermanager.HI   Uses $7CB0 to $95FF

DOS: A number of the routines make temporary patches to DOS while executing, but put them back when done. For this reason, avoid using the RESET button while one is executing. Try Ctrl-C instead. If you must RESET out of a SCAN, RELETE, INIT, FMTDSK, or CATALOG routine, DOS will probably be ruined, perhaps in some very subtle way. *Don't take chances, reboot.*

17

COMMAND PARSER

The Ampermanager Command Parser is invoked every time you execute an ampersand (&) command. This is the part of the program that figures out what command you want executed, and transfers control to the appropriate routine.

It is possible to "fool" the Command Parser because Applesoft stores all of its reserved words as one byte "tokens". Some of these tokens are the same as letters of the alphabet, and can get in the way of the Command Parser. Before going into some examples, here is a list of the ASCII to Applesoft equivalences that might cause you trouble:

ASCII	Applesoft
\<Ctrl-D\>	INPUT
\<Ctrl-G\>	READ
\<Ctrl-L\>	CALL
F	NOT
V	FRE
P	=

What this means is that if you type & V, *Ampermanager* will interpret it as & FRE. Some other examples are:

```
& NOT translates to & F
& REFRE translates to & REV
```

If strange things begin to happen, check these equivalences to see whether they might be the source of the problem.

18

ERROR MESSAGES

Ampermanager makes use of the error codes used by DOS and Applesoft. For a complete list of these codes, see Apple's *BASIC Programming Reference Manual* (page 136), and *The DOS Manual* (page 200).

These codes are left in location 222 (decimal), just as with Applesoft and DOS. The following is a table of error codes unique to *Ampermanager*:

CODE decimal	MESSAGE	POSSIBLE CAUSE
49	?DATA ERROR	Attempt to MOVE a string below $400.
		Error in the printer setup string for the &P command.
		Attempt to substitute too many characters into a string with an & LET command.
		Attempt to use the IN#$ command with an offset longer than the target string length.
212	NOT AVAILABLE	Attempt to scan a disk with more than 122 bad sectors or with the drive door open.
3	RANGE ERROR	This is a normal DOS error code, but there is a special meaning to it if it is generated by *Ampermanager*:
		Attempt to specify a track or sector number greater than that allowed in the VTOC sector in memory.

If you get this error, and cannot attribute it to DOS, you should try doing a CATALOG, or READing the VTOC sector to make sure your disk is valid.

| 176 | ?STRING TOO LONG ERROR | Besides its normal Applesoft use, an attempt to specify a printer setup string longer than 16 characters. |

19

INDEX OF COMMANDS